A Two Minute Forty Second Night

❖

Steven Ray Smith

FUTURECYCLE PRESS
www.futurecycle.org

Cover photo, "Light of the Ring" by Yamashita Yusuke; cover and interior design by Diane Kistner; Adobe Garamond Pro text and Josefin Sans titling

Library of Congress Control Number: 2021949553

Published by FutureCycle Press
Athens, Georgia, USA

ISBN 978-1-952593-29-1

To Neva, Sebastian, and Ivy

Contents

Coil

Towel-slap

I smelled a cigar while jogging

Be the

Coil

Coil

Us humans, we like a neatly coiled rope,
a kink-free hose around a hose reel,
data cords in a straight line from socket
to socket with no intertwining, and yet
our entire history is carefully
wrapping the Christmas lights in the crate
only to find a tangled mess next season.

Good spirits are always the plan,
especially when cruising the freeway with Taylor and Adele belting
it out crystal clear from the wireless.
But darn the cloverleaf with its on-ramps and off-ramps
too close together and always gridlocked
just before we make it home happy.
Darn our unremitting despair about the inevitable.

Topple

A bistro table loose at its base
is a hinge to my coffee and scone.
I cannot make this trivial breakfast
stop competing with me.

Panic is the hampering crux
of not being able to solve
the problem while not being able
to give it up.
I am here. I paid for it.
I steady it delicately while I wish so badly
it would topple over.

Accent wall

He told me a blue joke
just minutes ago, a risky joke
one only tells to a most trusted
friend. And she gave me half
her chicken-salad wrap, because she knows
I don't mind her cooties.
My buddy there simply nods
every time he sees me, as if we are thinking the same
thought, as if our accord is that firm.
All ten regard me like that.

Around the table, the ten-seat table
in the corner room, they only know
each other.

And now they are all laughing
at some private understanding.
I try to finish answering a question
one of them asked me in the hall, but
from the table her tickled eyes glance past me,
as if my navy blazer were some vague shadow
against the cadet-blue accent wall,

one of the many dark and uniform partitions
that give our corridor
its semblance of latitude.

The parlor

The old screen on its creaky hinges
sifted the pure aroma of camphor
from deep inside the doily darkness.
How soon would granny die
so I could stop reliving the requirements?

The tarnished handle would not pull.
Feet beyond the dim veil of motes,
just before the fade to nocturnality,
scraped toward me, then away,

but I was confused
about the requirements.
Don't forebears exit first? Why
was I the one locked outside?

I now can say: the requirements were a dainty
that the parlor was for me,
that the shambling inside was my decision.
I can now say for certain: the young
always exit the parlor first.

They are people in a line

They are simply people in a line.
Each one has his own elsewhere to be.
Their shoes have touched the grounds of clean and dirty
places in this town, but now a sign—
an arrow—points them forward through a tall
and winnowing rotunda to be assessed
for what each hopes will be his own success
but is, in truth, something very small.
The stanchion where the velvet rope arrives
does not care if one promotes his cuff links
or one his do-rag and does not know what fame
each knows outside the line. Each must abide
until his turn to answer in black ink:
What color are your eyes? What is your name?

Used to be

I used to line my birdcage with a thing called a newspaper.

Paper was ground up trees, a mash
dissolved in water, bleached, rolled flat, and dried.

News was baked tar
dissolved in mineral oil and slopped onto sheets
of metal then stamped upon those sheets of ground-up trees,
heretofore named paper.

The words were informative, coercive, tortious, banal, or false,
depending on the day or side of the paper you looked at.

When finished, the paper was thrown into a tub with onion
peels called a garbage can.

Onion peels, which looked similar to paper,
were the outer coating of a root used widely in flavoring
other foods.

Sometimes birds lived inside our homes.

These home birds were accustomed to humans and did not
fly away when approached. These birds lived in boxes
made of widely spaced metal bars so the human could see
the bird and the bird, the human.

Instead of throwing the paper in the garbage can,
some was used at the bottom of the bird's box, known as a cage,

because the bird, unlike the human, still defecated
the instant he needed to lighten his poisons.
The bird did not understand the basin of fresh, clean
water used by the humans because he considered fresh
water something for drinking and bathing.

Once the bird's scat fell upon the paper,
the paper was taken to the garbage
can or was sometimes reread if the scat
did not sully the words or their meaning.

If the bird's scat missed
the paper and hit the floor, the small wolf
called a Pomeranian would eat it, then find the basin of clean
water and drink.

Those were the days of newspapers
and all the funny things we did like
cut down trees and grind them up, read truth and falsehood
together, let birds and wolves live in our homes,
eat onions, throw words in the garbage, save poisons
in our bodies, splash fresh drinkable waters
with our own scat and never think
it would ever be
used to be.

Phantom

Yesterday I flailed
beyond proxemics,
me and my big mass of gaudy.
Watching you step back showed me
how brightly I thought I shined.

Today my arm throbs
with the pulse of nakedness.
I hunt for my catchpenny
pound, my free hand groping
for the preciousness that had only ever been
a pennyweight.

What happened was I let myself
dawdle on a towel for a simple hour,
laugh at nothing, feel you
joggling the bangle
and my palm and fingers with it.
The insouciant sand filches everything.

So there
it went,
and with it
yesterday's
emolument.

If you find it,
don't tell me.
Don't give it back.

Flurry

Your picture on the refrigerator has been there five years,
since the day it was taken.
Actually, the refrigerator itself was replaced once
but your picture stayed in its same position,
teaching us continuity and predictability.

Your unbroken grin and headband holding
a soft central part in permanent place were a permanent place
despite our rush-by flurries in the kitchen.

That was your message to our busy busy lives,
the life where swiftness was real,
like how swiftly you came back to celebrate another
birthday or new year or another anything with a picture of it.

If only we'd taken it in front of the moon.
We were moving too quickly to think:
The slow moon, as far as we know, never flurries away

A total eclipse of the sun

requires us to consider that a power
that's never left us
might

although we know it's just
a two minute, forty second
night.

You will see

They'll take your swivel chair away.
It wasn't yours anyway.

The coffee mugs will disappear
and come back only once a year.

The starting time and closing time
will start at nine and close at nine;

though nine to five with time to take
a twice-daily coffee break

and make new friends and buy a house,
convert one friend into a spouse,

were sort of promised, annual to annual,
though never listed in the manual.

When regulation comforts vanish,
the room at once appears outlandish,

and you'll feel foreign to yourself,
and think an itch betrays your health,

and yet you'll strain to stay in there,
despite the fact they took your chair,

because an inkling of who you were
means something normal could occur,

and you might reemerge unchanged,
your steps and tastes unrearranged.

Recall those years of rhythms and joys,
the lazy Thursdays and Friday noise.

Then leave your key upon the desk
and walk toward what will happen next.

Pause to greet your foreign you.
This backup you will act in lieu

of who you can no longer be.
It's also you, as you will see.

Towel-slap

Bait shyness

A pattering house mouse with itty pink ears,
the protagonist of a whole stack of cartoon baby books,
is now a giant hanta-tipped incisor,
its yellow claw of dentin axing
through the sheetrock, crunching away like almond bark.
It is unfazed by the hemorrhagic virus it hosts and spreads.

Despite how straightforward and polite it would be, poison
does not work.
For a mouse is wary of scrumptiousness on a place mat.
It knows what it sees: easy food is a ruse.
It will sample everything, but if anything
gastric happens it won't return, just keep undoing
the gypsum wallboard of our home.

The only way to stop it now is by a bald-faced face-off.
The fact that we don't relish exterminating the hero
we've heretofore known to be dressed in his smoking jacket,
reading a book in a mini wingback chair in the tiny living
room the other side of the mousehole,
does not make us weak citizens.
A compassion for pestilence is our best quality,
even as we do it.

Red-and-green

Doyen of the treetops
in his gaudy bespoke couture,
he was born under the talon-eye of raptors.
So where his gabby brainstorms
atop a knurly ribbonwood perch
in the back of the solarium present
him as a krewe-king of the canopies,
listen also to the chickadees
you can't make out and that don't
appease your syntax.
Then notice the tongue-tip
of your ever-present companion,
the spaniel, and how it wets its teeth.

Towel-slap

I knew you preferred peening
bronzes of beak, bovine, and barracuda
to idolizing me. That's why I said don't do it (rule two).
In order to protect you (rule one), I insisted
on being your main god (recognizing there are so many others).
The gilded calf, a golden Thoth,
an eighteen-carat
happily suffering Jesus beneath the top button of your blouse,
the precious padlock on a Birkin bag—
those charms I understood.
I knew you preferred shiny glistening shadows
to brooding cumuli
like me.

But I no longer know how to talk to you
when the god you now idolize is yourself.
My soulful rumbling inside a dark cloud is no longer enough.
I pray, as you towel-slap
the scrawny second string
known as every other nation
with your gigantic flag,
that you won't switch
me too.

Dear Epigraph

Thank you for your awesome
letters hovering over our small stature, stalwart,
etched into an entablature
that can weather any adversity,
by-and-by grimy from exhaust pipe soot,
tar and nicotine, and airborne French fry oil but always
power-washed anew for the next generation.

Thank you for giving us a thought
about ourselves that we love to think.

Dear Epigraph, likewise allow your colossus
to become quaint, crumble, kiss
the wrecking ball of change
when your "V" is no longer understood to be our "U"
and your Roman numerals are stick-figure cartoons—
when your wisdom has become a private
comfort to a private club
and your proverb
a shibboleth.

Why from the claw

Why, from his claw-foot chair,
a basis so heavy it has not moved in generations,
beside a grand fireplace with mown turf
in acres around that separate every gnarr
arising from the feral wilds, does he
order yet more protection?

When his father sat in the chair
and he sat upon his father's lap,
their sport, manners, jokes, recipes, and faith
were reiterations of peerage.

And now a dangerous gathering of questions
has amassed outside the huge fence surrounding the estate.
They pry him about his games, decorum, punchlines, palate,
and myside recitals.
They mistake him entirely.
He will not rebut what he does not know he intends.
Those are his rituals.
He is ritual.
Foreclosure is ritual.

Unpants

The town died,
though it still had its satellite
TV installer and grocery store—
both open.
The high school team still tried
to live up to the cheers in the bleachers, so the girls
would unpants with them after all the clocks went zero.

Why die if you're going to keep unpantsing?
I asked the town.

Why do you ask the question backward?
the town asked me.

And so we left it on those two open questions—
me not understanding that a hookup was still available
and the town not understanding that the pants
I'd worn upon departing
were still buckled neatly to my hips,
though the belt was a strip of something exotic,
like umlauts and the quincuncial map of the world.

On the way to the chancery

On the way to the chancery,
I fell and broke my outlook
into two jumbled screes
and blamed the chancery for it.

Which is right and which is wrong?
What is fair and what is not?
Who is sane and who is insane?
But I never reached the chancery
for Themis to tell me,
though I blamed her for not telling me.
Which cup of her confounding scale
the two pulverized heaps of me
tips down I may never know.

And this went on until you finally said listen—
I have neither blindfold nor sword.
I cannot listen dispassionately, nor can I fully judge you.
I don't know your answers, but I am not stone-still silent either.
My love and your outlook are the only telltales you have.
Believe them like they were actual answers.

I smelled a cigar while jogging

Freedom from want

In this freedom from want,
there is not a turkey
and not an apron
bowing before a cocked
father retrieving his prestige,
the carving set.

There is not a gray bun and bobby pins making way
for his magic upon her make-ready.
There are not children
fitful with hunger,
starched like dad,
fitful with convenience
and surveying the laughter while she
remains spackled in gravy.

In this version, she is hungry too.
He is still suited but seated.
She has likewise roasted, but there is a humorous part
and all around await her punchline.

Overlook

East Eleventh Street had the mephitis of transience
and guilty memories; that is, until its backroom
trick rooms became the best deal posh
money could buy. And so
East Eleventh Street became
the sidewalk for clear-skinned
graduates, their gadgets, their brewery
redolence, and their dogs.
No one remembers its origins,
as if the new balmy whiffs always were.

Then there is the Heights and its Private Road, not
too far away but up a very steep and segregating hill.
The residents had it declared a historic zone, meaning
it cannot change without consensus and permission, so
history has stopped in the Heights.

The third neighborhood is out there too, hard
to find, unnamed. It's the one where
the houses make rusty creaking noises, rodents
claim the crawl spaces, and paint flakes off constantly.
It's built on the edge of a granite overlook
with a panorama of the on-and-off
lights of the city.
It wants neither reinvention nor conservation
because its perspective is constantly focused
on the vibrancy below. And when people finally
discover it, they, like those already there,
won't even consider the quiet leaning of its timbers.

Our city

Back in the city with the all-night subways
and all that—
I'm sure your young city is just as energetic—
I was so relaxed,
finally having solved every question
except love and self-love, of course.

Now daily it's lights-out again so quickly
with not a single check having been marked
in the list I created way, way, way back.
It was the only thing I arrived carrying
to the great city.
She left a space for it in our super-stuffed
suitcase when we left.

You'll leave yours too
when you finally realize you'll never
be smart enough for it.
I thank her still for coming with me
and asking me no questions.

Courses

Most common is the loop,
a circuit from start to finish.
There is also the out-and-back, outing
to a distance and reverse.
In both, your friends will be exactly
where you left them, tending the ice chest.

Rarer is the point-to-point, start here and end
you don't know where.
The world's most storied,
the Boston and the Athens Classic, are these.
The crowds who waive you off will not see you finish.
Every step must be proven anew
to cheering sections that don't care
how your foregoing fans pepped you up or highballed the sky.
The only job: finish fast.

This passage is also a point-to-point.
Like the canon marathons, only the cadence
of your next footstrike matters and no
devotee will witness more than one.
The only difference: finish slow.

Cannonball

We're going to have to share
the driving if we want to make it
to the coast.

We exchanged simpers at Wheeling
and grew silently silent by Broken Arrow.
Toward Tucumcari
we were remote and separate existences
atop a common axle.

If there'd been a different choice
of partners or no race at all,
we'd both have chosen wiser
but missed the hilarity of the petrified forest:
permanently dead pines in the guise
of firewood for a soirée.

The leg through the Joshua trees
is our last chance to notice how rare all this is—
to maneuver how quickly a short race petrifies
into memory and just stops

or doesn't.

I smelled a cigar while jogging

Sunrise on the latex track at the junior
high, rounding the arc of the oval,
I drew in a breath upon a breath of sterile ozone.
My breathing was rhythmic with my ankles and the wind.
I was getting younger in the amnion of my neighborhood.
The buses arriving to start the day unloaded with the kids,
at once my seniors.

Then while opening my stride on the straightaway,
my heart a metronome to my jogging feet,
a runnel of gray fog drifted across the track from some
place the other side of the hedgerow,
and I stopped to inhale the

long-neglected sin.
Nothing, you see, equals the burning down of a thick, sun-
aged Oscuro.

Only after I'd sprinted into the blackthorn
and come out dripping profusely from the scratches
did I consider what I intended to say.
The neighbor with the cracked-clay face was going back inside,
so whether I meant to dare him for infringing my run
or ask him to share,
I could not; he was gone.

But all through the remaining morning
I was in a new mood
to be an old sinner who can no longer die,

and I would quit a job I did not hate
simply for not remembering why I couldn't.

A vertical line in the middle of a page

The left side is a panning squelch
from frontal, to parietal, to occipital,
acid house carried home in a bottle of Stolichnaya.
Oh it hurts, hurts, hurts, it oh, it oh, it oh, hurts, oh.
The trance resumes at midnight.

The right side is midnight as pirouette.
It is a sphere on a slightly tilted axis;
this is to recognize summer.
It is the mysterious 10,000 hours of practice,
the expertise to whirl and not fall.

The line is a frazzling poly lanyard
that upholds a massy finisher's medal.
It's the drizzly course of a spring marathon, run at 50.
It's the time bombast died quietly, at last.
It's the time death did not, though it could have.

Beginnings

An old sneaker splits a vent, and suddenly
it's shoe shopping day again;
or maybe it's not new shoes but the start
of the old foot finally going commando,
getting tough, calloused, human leather,
unsupple as a goat's horn.

Proper grammar and math parameters
say the finish comes after the start.
Songs and everyday witness tell the opposite.
The sun returns after a dark night,
the glory-fisted medalist is again democratically crouched
in his blocks,
the pisces we ate begat our energy to swim.
And this hopeful reversal:
one lived after dying, ended before beginning.
If it happened once, it can happen again.
We have sung and sung the hymn.

All we know or have ever known
is beginnings following endings.

Be the

Be the unicorn

Be the sum
of two forreals that equal a myth.
Screw the narwhal tusk to your forelock
and do not wonder why they are looking at you.
Of course they are, you oddity!
Remember also they are searching for you,
to decontaminate their water and reassure
themselves they are still virgins,
not the twofers they've been told and told themselves.
Thus they stammer.
They see the familiar in you but can't
figure how.

Be the candle

Conjure a halo in the empty cave
of an ordinary Tuesday night.
Cohere the faltering whispers into unmistakable vows.
Accompany a longful ask toward its prayer.
Illuminate a queen's gambit during a hurricane.
Be the power to destroy
an entire house yet magically
lower the volume and draw
the faces inward.

Be the unicyclist

Though strictly true, your claim's per se a lie.
Indeed, you ride a chair atop a chain,
a pinion and a splay of spokes, and by
a disembogue of creatine maintain
kinesiology via machine.
Contrasted to Achilles tugging plantar,
a foot traversing ground, you're what you mean
to be, a cyclist, a tour de force faster
than any marathoner, yet a fraud
according to the bicyclists who don
the ham-shank shorts and luminescent gaud—
vaudeville, unwelcome in the peloton.
Do not stop to hermeneuticize.
Their claims what you are not: those are the lies.

Be the good sybarite

The host will place you in the line.
It may be at the beginning, middle, or back.
You cannot request a move or trade places.

The price includes one plate and one trip.
More than one plate or trip are not allowed.
Most guests assume
this is up for discussion, but the answer
is always no.

You may eat whatever is available to you, but
if you have a good spot in line and eat all the sturgeon
there will be none left for those behind you.
These may include your own children.
You may feel this is alarmist, but please note:
there is no more sturgeon in the back.

If you eat only dessert, that's up to you.
Remember, you cannot go back through the line
if later you feel the emptiness of poor nutrition.
Once you leave the line, you're done.

Our disclosure: the buffet is a series of free choices, but
an empty chafing dish is as it appears.
Our advice: be a sybarite of good decisions.
Our summation: there is no back.

Be the color of your body

A single heel step
from the door behind,
so distinctly you—
bubble friend,
orange bubble,
not to touch.

In the dream you are
as purple as you are
leg to leg,
sanguine diadem,
stoplight mixed with midnight
through the window and negligee.

Your subcutaneous hand
cannot be not
shaken each entry into
your white rotunda.

If I'd met you without my eyes,
you'd be red phosphorous,
rivalrous allotrope
visible only in its test tube.

Single sliver of shade in thickets of scrub sumac,
you are the philosophical hue of a whole desert,
ultimate terrain of the entire earth.

Quackgrass

I am the quackgrass
growing from the concrete.
They paved over the light,
but I drank the water trapped
underneath with me
and broke through.

And now the concrete,
the pith of tombs,
hides my roots from the whacking wheels
and plastic whipcords
that weekly cut me back.

Each rejection
of my spindly striving leaves
makes my roots
woodier and wetter.

Make-do night

It's make-do night again at the bowling alley.

The fried pickles are dying
in the window like always while the orders keep churning—
soggy and cold with the batter sliding off.
There's a quick reheat

button on the microwave in the bar
that's a make-do solution but
really just a way to concentrate the staling
verjuice.

What other choices could we, should
we, make during those 30 ephemeral
seconds of the reheat timer?

For starters, let's not let the dinger sound,
like always, before
the answer.

Rich

Behind this door, ice cream
has double the calories
as behind that door,
but behind this door, it does not metabolize to fat.
Instead, it produces only luscious energy—
too much energy to experience, in fact—but never
becomes the subcutaneous inertia
of the mean
like the ice cream behind that door.

Visitors allowed entry to this door—
and most are not—
will experience the ice cream as something
extraordinary, when in fact they are missing the obvious—
or, more precisely, the obvious
hidden to all except to those who go there ordinarily.
And that is this:

this is that.

Jade

Volcanic come-out from mantle,
translucence and luminescence
forged with impregnability (except
by the master lapidist); we'll rush anew
to the bulletproof window to see the Mohs
perfect 10 debutante.

We fail to realize in the same showroom
is one we don't understand—
unfaceted with aboveground origins and a domed
silhouette that refracts a single color, its own.
It can be a knife, a Buddha, a bracelet, or
a cabochon in prongs for the richest wedding
that will at times be a knife, a Buddha, and a bracelet,
but never a first-time one-time hands-off
perfect debut.

Luxury lucent

And then one day,
the marble fortress with armored
windows at the corner of Profusion
Boulevard and Especial
Avenue sold a moment of lucent insight instead
of diamonds.

For an extraordinary occasion surpassing even
the summoning to fertility of the wedding,
the chronicling of survival in the birthday,
gratitude for fertility of the anniversary, and
the annulling of failures of the funeral,

they opened the hefty and segregating doors
and emptied onto the display case their lifetime savings
of begrudging tolerances, spurious excuses,
and self-serving deceptions in return
for a tiny box tied in ribbons
the jeweler slid across the glass.
They will never afford such luxury again.
But if they grasp how this can be—
an empty box, nothingness wrapped in preciousness—
they won't look to.

The small notches

An entire week and I finally rubbed
the last of the price tag's sticky residue
from the coffee mug I bought off the off-price rack.
At last, my fingers stretched around the warm
steel without cinching in the goop,
and that was the third notch for happiness.

Yesterday morning, I lost the little clip
that attaches my earphone cord to my lapel
and arrests the wire's tendency to strangle the scruff.
Then, suddenly, I spotted the tiny gray clamp on the gray
carpet, a jot of differentiation,
and that was the second notch for happiness.

The week began, as they do, at the drive-up.
I was two dimes short until I remembered
the accidental exchequer
beneath my car seat, an APR
of nickel dribbles from my pocket.
Sliding back the bucket, I found enough
for both the brew and a bonus shot of demitasse.
That was not the first notch, of course, just the hint
that set the iotas to accruing.

The Monday Bar

Shut off your screen and pack your things. Let's go!
It's happy hour at the Monday Bar.
Three quick pints and we'll be besting par
in tournaments we don't yet even know.
Monday's the day to celebrate what hasn't
happened, the triumph of everything that's yet
to come. And the dry mouth of regret
that trails a bingeing Saturday doesn't
beset our Tuesdays because Monday and all
that happens is a debt not due, not paid.
There's no use reciting gaffes we haven't made.
It's fruitless to scold the future after all.
What lingers is a heartbeat in the head.
The morning-after is a cadence ahead.

Median

This morning, I came to a hard stop,
meaning the lanes ahead were closed
for sweeping glass from the asphalt,
and I left my idling berlinetta
and walked into the house of God.

One important point:
I was only following a red bird that flew in there,
something to forget the impending reprimand for being late.
I did not realize it was the house of God
until my feet depressed in the morass,
so wild and soggy that a team of termites
were eating a fallen limb with no rush or deadline at all.
At first I thought, how can this wildness be so close
to our beautiful dysfunctional highway?

The response luxuriated behind me and overhead:
because it can, and it is!

The tilework

The tilework in the men's room is hexagons
floor to ceiling harmoniously set
by the mason on lime stucco and dried.
It's no accident it became the dry
and washable constant of a dirty place.

Likewise the honeycomb, its progenitor, is no accident—
a genius home, sweet genoise for others.

The product of a factor
cannot have more significant digits than the original.

Therefore, God exists.

Unsayable

A long week of words marching in,
marching in and out of a pillow,
the fuzzy sound of something going to happen,
a dim drum behind the glabella,
the drumbeat of some beseeching doubt
that starts fuzzy until it starts to roam
alongside a coughing feather about
the pitchy room grabbing random tomes
that sound like whispers from a holy ghost
who already knows the big answer.
This is the small moment when the most
deadlocked thing—time—allows the future.
Meet the he, she, it, they—
precisely the unsayable Yahweh.

Cicatrix

Undiscovered green ferns beside green
mosses beside fallen trees and towering trees
with hosanna branches high up toward the blue,

except there is one old oak at the boundary with a rusted strand
of barbed wire eight inches into its heartwood, at least 50 years
ingrown, such that removal requires cutting down the whole trunk.

It is an eyesore in this primordial shelter, though
the squirrels that climb the deep bark furrows
to their drey high in its crown deftly sidestep

the lockjaw spurs without pause.
Neither do their pups asleep in the dense canopy
second-guess that their nest is anything but the safest on earth.

Maybe the twanging fragment skewering its knot itches
the sapwood when the wind blows. Or maybe the cicatrix
is a handsome trophy of a lone sapling that thwarted the box-in

of the wildwoods, acorns still lying on the ground,
originality that required no improvement. The fragment twangs on.
What was a fence has blown to oxy-dust.

Bide

The meaning of life is death.
The meaning of Christianity is life
after death.
The profusion of words is to bide time.

Prayer

Let us be among the ones to be okay
Abba:
Us too.
We started here together but from different starts.
Oh yea, yea, yea,
like the singers say.

Let it be fair out there
Dios mio:
You can be first this time.
I did, I did, enjoy my time.
Oyez, oyez, oyez,
to the judges say.

Accept our feet,
Tellus Mater,
into your cool beach sand,
endlessly new to endless impressions.
kk:
the kindest way to say okay.

Amen

One day, there will be a paper to sign.
It will come stacked casually inside
the quotidian mail, its bold blank line
shuffled amid requests to be denied
or approved or simply tucked back in
until tomorrow. There was a big promise
you made when you decided to begin
this signal enterprise: it was not this.
Yet there you'll be, holding a stranger's pen,
hearing nothing but the carpet shift
with advisors and none to say *amen*
to your autograph and the rift
it will thereafter create. Now *you*
must say it. *You* must say it. *You. You.*

The language of flags

A lopping wind sock on a rusty staff does not lift a grommet,
does not clank the iron, does not wake the air traffic controller
in his single-wide to clear a visitor down to the desert
because there is no visitor; sunrise to sundown,
the sun revolves around a quiescent flag.

A jot west at the sunbelt metro hub,
checkers of five orange and four white squares reel
unflaggingly every degree of azimuths on a spindly stick-pole
from perpetual prop blasts, turbo blowbacks, and the wind itself.
Its herky-jerky says yes, construction of the new 10R/28L is in a rush,
opening soon to sprawl the sprawl—more planes, more.

Downtown, a mammoth new Old Glory
from its dickey box atop the bank tower
coachwhips the city below, driving the future.
Don't stop, don't rest, don't eat,
don't be European.

And at Base Camp before the Khumbu Icefall,
wind horses strung from poles to cairns
try to say you should not be here but, if you insist,
then listen to the language of flags:
hear and see here,
up there see, then breathe,
then nothing at all.

Acknowledgments

I would like to thank these journals where the following works in this collection first appeared, some in slightly different versions.

Bacopa Literary Review: "A vertical line in the middle of a page"
Barrow Street: "Bait shyness"
Beechwood Review: "Bide"
Blue Unicorn: "You will see"
The Broadkill Review: "Beginnings"
Chaleur Magazine: "Towel-slap," "Dear Epigraph"
The Dalhousie Review: "Jade"
ellipsis… literature and art: "Unpants"
Flapperhouse: "Luxury lucent"
Friends Journal: "The small notches"
Guesthouse: "The parlor"
HCE Review: "Be the good sybarite"
IHRAF Publishes: "On the way to the chancery"
The Kenyon Review: "They are people in a line"
Kudzu House Quarterly: "Median"
Light: A Journal of Photography and Poetry: "Rich"
Lines+Stars: "Topple"
The Literary Nest: "Amen"
The Maynard: "Phantom," "Courses"
New Madrid: "A total eclipse of the sun"
North Dakota Quarterly: "Overlook," "Make-do night"
Oxford Magazine: "Freedom from want," "Accent wall"
Plainsongs: "Our city"
Poet Lore: "Red-and-green"
San Pedro River Review: "Why from the claw"
Slice: "I smelled a cigar while jogging"
Southwest Review: "The language of flags"
Tales from the Forest: "Cicatrix"
Tar River Poetry: "Coil"
THINK: A Journal of Poetry, Fiction, and Essays: "Be the unicyclist"
Third Wednesday: "Be the unicorn," "Be the candle"
Tilde: "Be the color of your body"
The Timberline Review: "The tilework"
Windhover: "Unsayable" (published as "God's hour")
The Yale Review: "Used to be"

Acknowledgments

I would like to thank those journals where the following works in this collection first appeared, some in slightly different versions:

About FutureCycle Press

FutureCycle Press is dedicated to publishing lasting English-language poetry in both print-on-demand and Kindle formats. Founded in 2007 by long-time independent editor/publishers and partners Diane Kistner and Robert S. King, the press was incorporated as a nonprofit in 2012. A number of our editors are distinguished poets and writers in their own right, and we have been actively involved in the small press movement going back to the early seventies.

Each year, we award the FutureCycle Poetry Book Prize and honorarium for the best original full-length volume of poetry we published that year. Introduced in 2013, proceeds from our Good Works projects are donated to charity. Our Selected Poems series highlights contemporary poets with a substantial body of work to their credit; with this series we strive to resurrect work that has had limited distribution and is now out of print.

We are dedicated to giving all of the authors we publish the care their work deserves, offering a catalog of the most diverse and distinguished work possible, and paying forward any earnings to fund more great books. All of our books are kept "alive" and available unless and until an author requests a title be taken out of print.

We've learned a few things about independent publishing over the years. We've also evolved a unique and resilient publishing model that allows us to focus mainly on vetting and preserving for posterity poetry collections of exceptional quality without becoming overwhelmed with bookkeeping, mailing, fundraising activities, or taxing editorial and production "bubbles." To find out more about what we are doing, come see us at futurecycle.org.

The FutureCycle Poetry Book Prize

All original, full-length poetry books published by FutureCycle Press in a given calendar year are considered for the annual FutureCycle Poetry Book Prize. This allows us to consider each submission on its own merits, outside of the context of a traditional contest. Too, the judges see the finished book, which will have benefitted from the beautiful book design and strong editorial gloss we are famous for.

The book ranked the best in judging is announced as the prize-winner in January of the subsequent year. There is no fixed monetary award; instead, the winning poet receives an honorarium of 20% of the total net royalties from all poetry books and chapbooks the press sold online in the year the winning book was published. The winner is also accorded the honor of being on the panel of judges for the next year's competition; all judges receive copies of the contending books to keep for their personal library.

www.ingramcontent.com/pod-product-compliance
Lightning Source LLC
Chambersburg PA
CBHW070012100426
42741CB00012B/3214